HO HO HO!

TO:

_____

FROM:

_____

OCCASION:

_____

Merry Christmas, Y'all!

HI-PERFORMANCE

THERE'S NO PLACE LIKE
A MOBILE HOME
FOR THE HOLIDAYS

BY JEFF FOXWORTHY ⭐ ILLUSTRATIONS BY DAVID BOYD

RUTLEDGE HILL PRESS® · NASHVILLE, TENNESSEE · A DIVISION OF THOMAS NESLON, INC. · www.ThomasNelson.com

"Redneck 12 Days of Christmas" words and music by Jeff Foxworthy, James Scott
Rouse, Doug Grau, and Timothy C. Wilson © 1995 Max Laffs Publishing, Inc.
(BMI), Shabloo Music (BMI), Boo N Bing Music (BMI), Wilson & DiPetta
Publishing (ASCAP) (Administered by MCS America, Inc.). All Rights Reserved.
International Copyright Secured. Used by Permission.

"'Twas the Night After Christmas" by Jeff Foxworthy © 1997 Jeff Foxworthy.
Arranged and produced by James Scott Rouse and Doug Grau. All Rights
Reserved. International Copyright Secured. Used by Permission.

Published by Rutledge Hill Press, a Division of Thomas Nelson, Inc.,
P.O. Box 141000, Nashville, Tennessee 37214.

Design by Anderson Thomas Design, Inc.
www.andersonthomas.com

ISBN 1-4016-0194-4

Printed in the United States of America

05 06 07 08 — 5 4 3 2

INTRODUCTION

I've read that Christmas is a very depressing time of year for some people. My guess is that family get-togethers have a lot to do with that. Watching Uncle Ned dip his fingers in the onion dip and realizing that you two share DNA is enough to make Pollyanna depressed.

Personally, I consider the holiday season a great time to gather new material. It's like hunting a baited field: decorations from beer companies and taxidermists, presents from yard sales, outfits that would embarrass Madonna, and more bad jokes than you'd hear at an accountants' convention.

For those of you who favor traditional Christmases, I've included in this book the "Redneck 12 Days of Christmas" and my own "Twas the Night After Christmas." There's sure to be somebody at your get-together who can read without help, and after the eggnog is served, plenty of people will be willing to sing.

So sit back, enjoy the fun, and have a very redneck Christmas!

JEFF FOXWORTHY

YOU MIGHT BE A REDNECK IF...

You made the kids cry by painting a red nose on the deer head hanging in your living room.

AYEiii!!

YOU MIGHT BE A REDNECK IF...

You serve the Christmas turkey on a platter bearing Dale Earnhardt's picture.

YOU MIGHT BE A REDNECK IF...

Your Christmas tree came from an interstate median. **7**

YOU MIGHT BE A REDNECK IF...

Your nativity scene has people wearing camouflage.

YOU MIGHT BE A REDNECK IF...

THE NEIGHBORS START A PETITION
OVER YOUR CHRISTMAS LIGHTS.

YOU MIGHT BE A REDNECK IF...

YOU USE A BUG LIGHT AS A CHRISTMAS DECORATION.

YOUR KIDS' CHRISTMAS LETTER TO SANTA
INCLUDED THE WORDS ". . . OR ELSE."

YOU SHOT MISTLETOE OUT OF THE TREES IN YOUR YARD.

YOU GAVE YOUR WIFE A
GLUE GUN FOR CHRISTMAS.

You might be a redneck if...

You've ever shot a partridge out of a pear tree.

YOU MIGHT BE A REDNECK IF...

For Christmas you gave your wife a homemade fur coat.

YOU MIGHT BE A REDNECK IF...

YOU TAKE THE FAMILY CHRISTMAS
SHOPPING AT A YARD SALE.

YOU MIGHT BE A REDNECK IF...

Santa Claus refuses to let your kids sit in his lap.

You might be a redneck if...

Your Christmas tree has a deer stand in it.

REDNECK 12 DAYS OF CHRISTMAS

Jeff Foxworthy, James Scott Rouse, Doug Grau, and Timothy C. Wilson

Friend: WHOA! Somebody done been to the Wal-Mart!

Jeff: No, man. This is just the stuff I got for Christmas.

Friend: You cleaned up! Whatcha get?

Choir: FIVE FLANNEL SHIRTS . . .

Jeff: FOUR PIEDMONT TIRES,
THREE SHOTGUN SHELLS,
TWO HUNTIN' DOGS,
AND SOME PARTS TO A MUSTANG GT.

Friend: Jeff, I think you got gypped. There's TWELVE days to Christmas!

Jeff: I know that. I got it covered. Look over there in the corner.

Friend: That's yours, too?!?

Jeff: Yeah . . .

TWELVE-PACK OF BUD,

ELEVEN RASSLIN' TICKETS,

"TEN" OF COPENHAGEN,

NINE YEARS PROBATION,

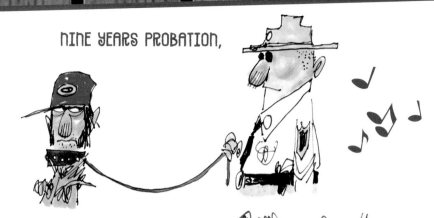

EIGHT TABLE DANCERS,

SEVEN PACKS OF RED MAN,

SIX CANS OF SPAM . . . (WHEW).

FIVE FLANNEL SHIRTS . . .

FOUR PIEDMONT TIRES,

THREE SHOTGUN SHELLS,

TWO HUNTIN' DOGS,

AND SOME PARTS
TO A MUSTANG GT.

Friend: Man, them ain't normal Christmas presents.

Jeff: Naw, they're redneck gifts.

Friend: Redneck gifts?

Jeff: Yeah, you know. Like if you bought your wife earrings that double as fishing lures. Or if you can burp the entire chorus of "Jingle Bells."

Friend: What's wrong with that?

Jeff: I didn't say there was anything wrong with it, but it's hard to beat . . .

TWELVE-PACK OF BUD,

ELEVEN RASSLIN' TICKETS,

"TEN" OF COPENHAGEN,

NINE YEARS PROBATION,

EIGHT TABLE DANCERS,

SEVEN PACKS OF RED MAN,

SIX CANS OF SPAM . . . (WHEW).

Choir: FIVE FLANNEL SHIRTS . . .

Jeff: FOUR PIEDMONT TIRES,

THREE SHOTGUN SHELLS,

TWO HUNTIN' DOGS,

AND SOME PARTS TO A MUSTANG GT.

Friend: You know, you can't really consider it a Christmas
'les you go down to the penitentiary 'n visit yer mama.

Jeff: You're not listening to me . . . Get the car key out of your ear.
That's where the "nine months probation" comes in.
I'm gonna do it for ya again . . . Now listen . . .

Jeff:
TWELVE-PACK OF BUD,
ELEVEN RASSLIN' TICKETS,
"TEN" OF COPENHAGEN,
NINE YEARS PROBATION,
EIGHT TABLE DANCERS,
SEVEN PACKS OF RED MAN,
SIX CANS OF SPAM . . .

Choir: FIVE FLANNEL SHIRTS . . .

Jeff:
FOUR PIEDMONT TIRES,
THREE SHOTGUN SHELLS,
TWO HUNTIN' DOGS,
AND SOME PARTS TO A MUSTANG GT.
. . . Are you cryin'?

Friend: (Sniff) No, it's just my allergies.

Jeff: Happy holidays, everybody.

29

Christmas dinner was too slow crossing the road on Christmas Eve.

You might be a redneck if...

Your Christmas tree is still up in February.

You might be a redneck if...

You string Christmas lights on the antlers
of the deer mounted above your fireplace.

YOU MIGHT BE A REDNECK IF...

YOUR CHRISTMAS PRESENT TO YOUR WIFE WAS GETTING THE SEPTIC TANK PUMPED.

YOUR TOWN PUT THE NEW GARBAGE TRUCK IN THE CHRISTMAS PARADE.

YOU THINK POINSETTIA IS A TYPE OF BIRD DOG.

33

You might be a redneck if...

Christmas dinner was ruined because you ran out of ketchup.

YOU MIGHT BE A REDNECK IF. . .

You decorate your tree with pop-tops and pickled eggs.

You might be a redneck if...

Your mother has "ammo" on her Christmas wish list.

You might be a redneck if...

The centerpiece for the Christmas dinner table was prepared by a taxidermist.

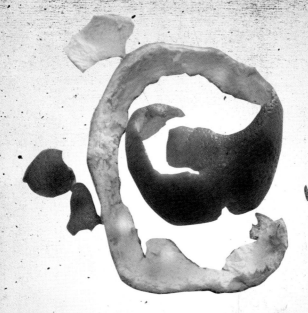

You might be
a redneck if...

YOU THINK ORANGE PEELS LEFT ON THE
COFFEE TABLE ARE HOLIDAY POTPOURRI.

You might be a redneck if...

You've ever wrapped a Christmas present in aluminum foil.

You MIGHT BE A REDNECK IF...

YOUR PAWNSHOP SENDS YOU A CHRISTMAS CARD.

DURING CHRISTMAS DINNER, YOU DO YOUR IMPRESSION OF A DOG CHOKING ON A CHICKEN BONE.

IN YOUR CHURCH'S CHRISTMAS PLAY, TWO OF THE WISE MEN WERE SMOKING.

YOU BOUGHT YOUR WIFE'S CHRISTMAS PRESENT AT THE GUN & TACKLE SHOP.

You might be a redneck if...

Even your snowman has a beer gut.

YOU MIGHT BE A REDNECK IF...

You've ever made a Christmas wreath out of a tire.

You MIGHT BE A REDNECK IF...
YOU DECORATE YOUR DOG FOR CHRISTMAS.

YOU MIGHT BE A REDNECK IF...

You've ever served Christmas dinner
on a Ping-Pong table.

You might be a redneck if...

The plastic deer in your yard at Christmas double as practice targets.

YOU MIGHT BE A REDNECK IF...

You stand under the mistletoe at Christmas and wait for Granny and Cousin Sue-Ellen to walk by.

'Twas the Night After Christmas

Jeff Foxworthy

'Twas the night after Christmas and all through the trailer,
  The beer had gone flat and the pizza was staler.
The tube socks hung empty, no candies or toys.
I was camped out on my old La-Z-Boy.

The kids they weren't talking to me or my wife.
The worst Christmas, they said, they had had in their lives.
My wife couldn't argue and neither could I,
So I watched TV and my wife she just cried.

When out in the yard the dog started barkin'.
I stood up and looked and I saw Sheriff Larkin.
He yelled, "Roy, I am sworn to uphold the laws
And I got a complaint from a feller named Claus."

I said, "Claus? I don't know nobody named Claus,
And you ain't taking me in without probable cause."
Then the sheriff he said, "The man was shot at last night."
I said, "That might have been me. Just what's he look like?"

The sheriff replied, "Well, he's a jolly old feller, with a big beer gut belly
That shakes when he laughs like a bowl full of jelly.
He sports a long beard and a nose like a cherry."
I said, "Sheriff, that sounds like my wife's sister Sherri."

"It's no time for jokes, Roy," the sheriff he said.
"The man I'm describing is dressed all in red.
I'm here for the truth now—it's time to come clean.
Tell me what you've done, tell me what you've seen."

Well, I started to lie, then I thought, what the hell,
It wouldn't be the first time I spent New Year's in jail.
I said, "Sheriff, it happened last night about ten.
I thought that my wife had been drinking again.

"When she walked in from work, she was white as a ghost.
I thought maybe she had seen one of them UFOs,
But she said that a bunch of deer had just flown over her head
And stopped on the roof of our good neighbor Red.

"Well, I ran out to look and the sight made me shudder,
A freezer full of venison standing right on Red's gutter.
Well, my hands were a-shakin' as I grabbed my gun,
When outta Red's chimney this feller did run.

"And slung on his back was this bag overflowin'.
I thought he'd stolen Red's stuff while old Red was out bowlin'.
So I yelled, 'Drop it, fat boy, hands up in the air!'
But he went about his business like he hadn't a care!

"So I popped off a warning shot over his head.
  Well, he dropped that bag and he jumped in that sled,
And as he flew off I heard him extort,
  'That's assault with intent, Roy, I'll see you in court.'"

The End

YOU MIGHT BE A REDNECK IF...

You've ever gift-wrapped a tire.

YOU MIGHT BE A REDNECK IF...

YOU HAVE A TURKEY DECOY ON CHRISTMAS LAYAWAY.

YOU GET ODOR-EATERS AS A CHRISTMAS PRESENT.

YOU'VE EVER REUSED CHRISTMAS CARDS.

YOU HANG CHRISTMAS ORNAMENTS WITH PAPER CLIPS.

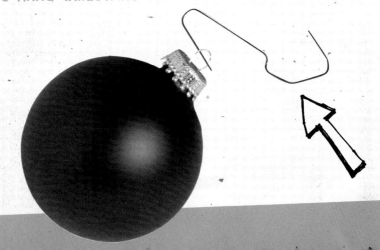

You might be a redneck if...

You've ever left Santa Claus a PBR and a Slim Jim.

You might be a redneck if...

You've ever done your Christmas shopping at a truck stop.

THE END